T0064735

SKIPPING EASTER

LAWRENCE M. VENTLINE, D.MIN.

authorHOUSE®

AuthorHouse™
1663 Liberty Drive
Bloomington, IN 47403
www.authorhouse.com
Phone: 1-800-839-8640

Published by AuthorHouse 1/29/2013

ISBN: 978-1-4817-0828-9 (sc)
ISBN: 978-1-4817-0827-2 (e)

Library of Congress Control Number: 2013901219

To

Kenneth Untener

A Breath of Fresh Air

FOREWORD

By Bishop Thomas J. Gumbleton, D.D.
Detroit, Michigan
January 17, 2013

This story about Skipping Easter had me wondering at first, but, when I began reading the short, simple but so human anecdotes that run through the book, I began to see how things are not always as they seem. Like Easter, and Father Larry Ventline's proposal to skip it this year. Then, he draws the reader into the importance of celebrating the Holy Week events of Holy Thursday, Good Friday, the Easter Vigil and Easter Sunday.

His thought about going to Easter Island near Chile, for Easter is fascinating but hardly enough for him to finally skip Easter, after all.

The stories here connect us with the city where he grew up and which he loves. It is easy to remember with him the streets and neighborhoods, factories and schools, ethnic and racial groups and all the vibrant life of Detroit in the last five decades.

The stories are so very human. But there is always a presence of God in them because the author lives in that presence himself and all that he experiences in events and people necessarily includes an active awareness that God is part of everything and everyone in our life. Without realizing it immediately we discover as we read these stories that we are being provided with spiritual guidance and nourishment.

Sometimes, I am sure, we all need explicit and very straight forward spiritual direction. But for an easy and gentle intrusion of the spiritual into our lives we could not find anything much better than connecting with the people, events, issues, and need to celebrate the Easter season that Fr. Ventline writes about. As we read, we find ourselves moving with him into rich spiritual reflections.

I hope that many people manage to discover this book dedicated to the late Bishop Ken Untener who worried about our culture and time losing the Triduum of Holy Week.

"Coaches can get too focused on results and winning, so it's good to step back and let go of things a little bit. I just try to change the things I can, accept the things I can't, and pray I have the wisdom to know the difference between the two. I follow three rules: Do the right thing, do the best you can, and always show people you care."

- Lou Holtz, Head Coach at Notre Dame

ALSO BY LAWRENCE MATTHEW VENTLINE, D.MIN.

A Dump, a Garden, and One's Worth: Growing An Interior Life,

Masculine Spirituality: Male Soul Stuff,

Anger: Reminders for Raging Times,

Gratitude: Reminders When Ungratefulness Sets In,

Guardinan of Your Soul: A Class in Acceptance (Notes of Edward D. Popielarz),

Soul Stuff: A Class in Acceptance Workbook,

A Pearl A Day: Wise Sayings for Living Well,

Stormy, Stilling Stories: Confessions of a Parish Priest,

Story Hungry: Roots, Relationships, Reflections,

Securing Serenity in Troubling Times: Living One Day at a Time

Cries of the People: Ministry Matters Mostly Personal with Practical Hints, Helps and Stories to Savor,

A Dump, A Fresh Garden, and One's Worth (Family-Illustrated Edition),

The Witness Value of the Visit of Pope John Paul II to Detroit, MI., USA: Its Meaning and Message, and,

Tale So True of My Chrismas Tree: Everything Belongs In Our World.

INTRODUCTION

My twin sister, Patti, and I, must have skipped home from Lynch School on Palmetto Street near Van Dyke Avenue faster that day than most. In fact, he would have been proud of how we learned to appreciate exercise from dad's quick clip walking everywhere. Our little feet struggled to keep up. This day, however, there was a run in our skip if you can imagine that. Dad was not at our kindergarten classroom door at his usual time to walk us home that 12 noon day. We were frightened. Dad was always there. What happened? Is he OK? In fact, once we reached our two-story aluminum-sided home on Detroit's east side near the City Airport, we rushed to the couch with our blanket covering us as we huddled together. Fear works that way. The long wait began. It was something we would have liked to skip.

Hours must have past. And, hours. Finally, Aunt Gertie arrived with Better Made Potato Chips, ice cream, and more. Mom's sister from the merged side of her family from Cheboygan, MI., was always bringing surprises to the seven of us kids while both parents worked much of the day outside our home. They had to, they said. To make ends meet, mom worked part time at Pilgrim Laundry on Mt. Elliott, while dad worked the midnight shift at the Plymouth Automobile Plant on Lynch Road, a block from where the nine of us resided until the civil unrest in Detroit in the late 60s. Cars, the Supremes, and I heard Hamtramck's toilet seat manufacturing site made Motown, Michigan, famous. For his morning or afternoon shift at the Budd Company, dad would leave early to catch the DSR bus to St. Jean and Mack. How dad kept that schedule, I don't know. When cars were yet not the lone king in town, I remember riding a trolley and watching the sparks from the electric lines overhead, My mother and I seemed to enjoy the ride to Herman Kiefer Hospital to get me tested for tuberculosis that seemed to have a history on my dad's side of his large merged families from Port Austin, in Michigan's thumb area. Both dad and mom left their homes as teens to earn some money to help support them while setting up homesteads here in the metropolitan area near Medbury at Mt. Elliott, and, not far from Saint Hyacinth Church on Farnsworth at McDougall.

While we waited for the bus on Van Dyke for our two-mile ride to Harper where we exited the bus that was a stone's throw from Saint Thomas the Apostle School, we couldn't wait for Friday mornings. The aroma filled the entire Polish neighborhood, let alone our own noses. In fact, that's all we would talk about waiting for the bus daily. After all, dad seemed to be the one whom skipped out of work by 6 am to pick up home-made cakes from the bakery at the bus stop. It was a treat.

You must be wondering why I would skip Easter this year. First of all, I skipped Christmas Day. Really. After Mass I went straight home to bed wondering how I made it through the fifty-five-minute service in Hamtramck at Our Lady Queen of Apostles Church on Conant, north of Canfiff Avenue. Hamtramck must be the most diverse city in the world with Middle Easterners, South Asians, and a variety of other ethnic groups in a town with a population like that of Harrison Township where I live. But, the faces and faiths of the 30,000 residents have changed from a Polish enclave where people came from their native homeland to work at the Dodge Plant.

Skipping Christmas and dinner at my sister, Marcy's and Bruce's home in Romeo, was not in the plan that Christmas Day. I recalled the book, Skipping Christmas, by John Grisham. It follows the fortunes of Luther Krank, and his wife, Nora, attempting to skip Christmas altogether with a getaway vacation. Their daughter Blair is doing volunteer work in Peru. So, they will save the cash they'd spend on the Christmas event by hastening off on a Caribbean cruise. No doubt, I entertained similar thoughts given all the hustle and bustle and stress of expectations and preparations for the 'perfect' holiday season. And, skipping Easter sounds like just what the doctor ordered for this year, March 31, 2013. Like the Kranks who checked the costs on their computer spreadsheets. Tally showed $6,100, while a top-of-the-line cruise for two was $5,000! Cruising the seas and skipping Christmas has Mr. Krank already imagining bikini-clad bronzed girls everywhere on the hot and sandy, sunny beaches.

With tongue and cheek dry wit, the brief tome shows that nothing is as it seems. Skipping anything may just work in reverse. Take, for example, the prolific pastor and best-selling author, Andrew Greeley's story of a woman in Bethlehem, named Babushka. She kept the cleanest and neatest house in town and was also the best cook, neighbors reported. Rumors of the Magi arriving in town reached her but she paid no attention. She just kept on working. A cavalcade of riders with pipes ringing out and drums blaring caused Babushka to look out her window. After all, the richly-dressed kings were coming toward her home. They said they came to honor the little prince who had been born in Bethlehem. They asked her for beds and breakfasts.

Babushka cooked a delicious meal for them, remade all the beds, and, wore herself out.

The following morning the kings begged her to come with them so she too might see the little prince. She said she would follow them soon. Once she finished the dishes, and swept the kitchen floor, and washed the windows, and wiped off the table. She even cleaned the house again and retrieved some toys from a cabinet that her own little prince played with decades ago, but died years ago. She had no more need of them and would give them to Jesus. She put them in a basket by the door, and, sat down for a few moments of rest before following the wise men.

Hours later, however, she awakened, grabbed the toys, and rushed into town. But the kings were gone and so were the little prince and his parents. Ever after, it is noted, Babushka has followed after them. Whenever she finds a new born babe, she looks to see if he is the little prince. Even if he or she is not, the aging Babushka leaves a toy for the child. Perhaps she finally found the prince, but, also learn a lesson: Never let the important interfere with the essential. You may say she simply skipped the chance of a lifetime to visit the prince. Work and other matters got in the way. Another lost opportunity, even though her hospitality to the kings, among others, was remarkable.

I remember in high school when I almost skipped football and basketball. After all, work at the ice cream parlor and my brother Lucas' hand-me-down cemetery tombstone marker job kept this guy busy. Yet, wanting to be popular and accepted in my teen years, I did what I had to in order to make it to practice. Double sessions in the summer for football practice prevented me from regular attendance. And, when school started up in September in 1966, Jim Nesbitt, the coach told Bob Smith and me in no uncertain terms to be out on the field after the pep rally in our cracker-box gym at Saint Thomas. I recall our helmets crashing head on into each other's before practice started.

Never did I skip sessions again. In fact, playing for the evening opener at Jayne Field on Charles Street was a highlight for me. After getting plowed over by the mighty Crusaders of Saint Clement High School in Center Line, MI., I rose again and again. Still, I missed a touchdown pass by inches.

Skipping Easter this year would also recall the Velveteen Rabbit, a touching story of a stuffed toy rabbit which is loved so much by his boy that he becomes real. As real as the resurrection, as suffering, dying and rising as the paschal package for believers. Those mysteries that I'd win some and lose some in life that I wouldn't get everything I wanted, that I would be passed over in a job promotion, could be rejected by a first love or the tight-knit group at school, and, one day would get seriously ill, even die eventually. These all thrust forth like the forceful rush of flowing water overhead in a shower each day. Skipping Easter would bring all these memories forth. Skipping Easter? What a proposal? Where did such an idea come? I started to look over my shoulder now. Wonderment filled me about who was stirring this trouble within? Who?

ONE

Although some days I wanted to skip the Detroit Public School mentor reading program, I reported given that a commitment is to be kept and honored. Reading the Velveteen Rabbit to students at the school on Marseilles on the border of Grosse Point was a cherished hour each week. The little readers like this story of the little Velveteen Rabbit that was given to a British lad at Christmas and then left in a toy cupboard, unloved and unwanted. Aren't all toys like that once they make their debut for a few minutes? I know I'd tire easily of the same toys, trains, or trucks. Now, chasing down and drowning out chipmunks from their holes in Forest Lawn Cemetery, or, at Mount Olivet, just north of McNichols at Van Dyke - that gave a thrill, a 'high,' a buzz to my older brother, Bob, and, our harem of friends, including Ray, John, Eddie, and more. Bob wasn't one to skip capturing a pigeon or two, among a plethora of other animal friends to raise. He always seemed to have a makeshift cage set up for any passing critter who dared to take the bait inside it. In fact, he loves nature so much in Port Austin that he resides there near Jenks Park. No skipping here for a bird in the pot!

The Velveteen Rabbit has its sage, Skin Horse. He is so old now that his brown coat has gone bald in patches, and his tail hairs were pulled for stringing beads. Go figure. Skin Horse witnessed a procession of mechanical toys come and go in the nursery. Some were broken when they left, forever to be toys. The sage tells the rabbit, however, that the toy which is loved by a child will someday become real.

"Does it hurt?" asked the rabbit.

"Sometimes," shouted Skin Horse to Rabbit. He always told the truth that set him free! "When you are Real you don't mind being hurt...by the time you are Real, all your hair has been loved off, and your eyes drop out and you get loose in the joints and very shabby. But these things don't matter at all, because once you are Real, you can't be ugly, except to people who don't understand."

Once upon a time in this same rabbit story, the boy's nanny is unable to locate the china dogs that always go to bed with him. So, hurriedly, she snatches the first toy her hand fetches in the cupboard, the Velveteen Rabbit.

"Here," she quietly says, "take your old Bunny! He'll do to sleep with you!" And she dragged the Rabbit out by one ear, and put him in the Boy's arms.

Nights after the Rabbit still slept in the Boy's bed like a committed spouse does in holy matrimony. But, initially, he felt uncomfortable. He would roll over on him, hug him tight, and even push him under the pillow so far that the Rabbit gasped for air. Soon, however, Rabbit liked it since the Boy talked with him. He even made tunnels for him beneath his pajamas. Like burrows that rabbits stayed in, the Boy wanted Rabbit to be at home. Both played games. As the night light illumined in the dark, the Boy fell asleep. Then, Rabbit snuggled down under Boy's warm chin. Rabbit also dreamed while Boy's hand gripped Rabbit through the night.

Happiness pervaded for Rabbit. Time flew. And, his tail stitches got shabby and parted, and, the pink wore off his nose where the Boy kissed him.

"And once, when the Boy was called away suddenly for tea, the Rabbit was left out on the lawn...and Nana had to come and look for him with the candle because the Boy couldn't go to sleep unless he was there...And Nana grumbled as she rubbed him off with the corner of her apron. "You must have your old Bunny,!" she said. "Fancy all that fuss for a toy!"

The Boy sat up in bed and stretched out his hands. "Give me my Bunny!" he said. You mustn't say that! He isn't a toy. He's REAL!" Little Rabbit was happy to hear that. He knew what the Skin Horse spouted was true. He was no longer a toy. He was Real. The Boy said it.

The Boy falls into scarlet fever. It's one of those Easter mysteries I mentioned earlier. Sickness and suffering are part of the package of life's dying and rising. Rabbit is mocked by the real rabbits where Rabbit sits in the garden unmoved now.

Rabbit misses the Boy, and the sage Skin Horse, and the inner house of the nursery.

"Of what use was it," the Rabbit weeps, "to be loved and lose ones beauty and to become real if it all ended like this?" A tear rolls down his worn velvet nose, lands on the ground, and, a flower bursts forth with a golden cup. As the blossom opens up, a beautiful Fairy steps out. She takes the Rabbit into her arms and kisses him. She is the nursery magic Fairy, who comes for the toys when the children finish playing with them. She rescues them and keeps them resurrected and REAL!

What spontaneously emerged in my mind as I reflected on Rabbit, were one woman's recent and daily wrestling with life, the death she would have loved to skip, and her final breath eventually that silenced her. "What for?" asked Eleanor Josaitis from her bed. Born on December 17, 1931, and moved from Taylor, MI., to Berkley Street near Seven Mile/ Livernois, she was the wife of Don, mother of five, and, the co-founder of Detroit's Focus:HOPE with the late Father William Cunningham in 1968 after Detroit's civil unrest. Josaitis died August 9, 2011 in the Angela Hospice in Livonia, MI., after repeated risings from threats to her life, and, ringings of evergreen hope in a life lived well and fully. Her question about life's meaning to me on her dying bed, and life's end, came when I applauded yet another award or trophy she earned as she tirelessly recognized the dignity and beauty of every person, pledged intelligent and practical action to overcome racism, poverty and injustice, and, to build a metropolitan Detroit community where all people may live in freedom, harmony, trust and affection (Focus:HOPE Mission Statement).

TWO

"I know your streets, sweet city, I know the demons and
angels that flock and roost in your boughs like birds. I know
you, river, as if you flowed through my heart. I am your
warrior daughter. There are letters made of your body as
a fountain is made of water. There are languages of which
you are the blueprint and as we speak them the city rises."

                                                    –Elka Cloke

S kip that.

Glass, marble and mirrors have their way reflecting so much of life's
consolation and desolation, ups, down, roller-coaster-like ride that envelopes
one trek, limited as it is like a blade of grass that passes, as the writer of the
Psalms of the Good Book notes. The spiritual life is like that. We carry it
like we carry sexuality, physicality, and being. We are all of them integrated
into one with the ultimate One who made us in this one world we are
in atonement with always in our walk before we are silent and pass over.

Skip that boulder, I said, as gardeners worked around that shiny, earth-toned, and wore out rock that reflected our faces, let alone the faith we followed to a plot of land where builders began what they could not finish. At least for now the condominium complex they started a decade ago is left unfinished.

Some things are better left alone. Skip it. Skip that.

Before a dump grew up with clutter and debris across the street from where I live now, in the beginning was a Garden of Paradise (Genesis 2:8), so to speak. Another garden is found in Saint John's Gospel (John 18:1) across the Kidron Valley which Jesus and his disciples used.

Finally, there is another garden, "in which no one had yet been buried. So they placed Jesus there (John 19:41-42).

My seminary classmate, Kenneth Kaucheck, reviewed my, A Dump, A Garden, And, One's Worth: Growing An Interior Life.

Kaucheck, notes that there is plenty of material here with plenty of scope for digesting, but, the issue of the garden does not monopolize the book. It is not preoccupied with the fall from grace in the Garden of Eden. It is not centered in the agony in the garden in which Jesus prays that he may not have to drink from the cup he'd rather skip. Nor it is about the garden of his burial from which the Resurrection is proclaimed.

Instead of being about gardens, it's more about dumps, in an imaginative way, as pastoral care minister and acquaintance Jo Ann Loria describes the story. It is about growing an interior life of prayer, of connection with the Creator, of an inner life. It's about the Garden of Paradise that God created and placed humanity in and we then in turn began to turn it into a dump. A dump is the opposite of a garden that hatched from inattention and garbage strewn upon its original beauty. Call it original sin, or, missing the mark, from the Greek, "harmatia." Like the archer who fails to aim for the target, skips it, you may say, misses the mark. Sin, separation and alienation from God is like that.

My dump story calls to mind the boss in Zorba the Greek by Nikos Kazantzakis. "If only I could never open my mouth ...until the abstract idea had reached its highest point, and, had become a story," says Kazntzakis.

What creates a dump of one's life, of God's Good Earth given to us for a limited time with work and rent to pay as the price we pay for inhabiting it with care as Mahatma Gandhi reportedly said, is neglect and indifference. It is a frozen heart that kills and destroys natural and physical life in and outside the womb, on battle fields, within conflicted and divided allegiances, and beyond. Evil starts within despite the blaming that engages excuses so often.

Over time, however, attention and affection, invites healing, recovery and union with the One world. It is restored to its garden-like state, its original condition over time. It's like people who treat themselves like a dump without esteem, dignity, and God-given worth.

That's how people tend to relate with them, then. It's chemistry, attraction for the similar. Goodness begets more of the same. Dumps attract similar stuff, sad to admit, until the cycle of violence is stopped. When it ends, life begins again far from the trauma and terror pervading the globe with gunshots everywhere it seems these days. I can skip those deadly weapons of mass destruction, having had to duck a few bullets in my seven decades on board here.

Life's twists and turns, desolation and consolation comprise the trek and trail of the years one has on earth from the moment of birth.

Every pilgrim has his or her story to tell. Tales of sorrow and joy, and more. However long the years, like my own path born of farmer parents who taught me how to be practical and industrious. A paternal twin with Patti, sibling to six others, including my brother, Lucas who was killed in Vietnam in '68, shy and introverted the first half of my life, raised in a Polish parish and neighborhood, blessed with a father who experienced the death of his own birth mother when he was only six months old.

When James Carroll was exiting as a chaplain at Notre Dame University, and, a priesthood he seemed to love, I was embracing it in 1975 when I was ordained a deacon. My own soul's breakdown in '85 I could have skipped, but, how would I have learned life's lessons and love? There are no accidents, I believe. God is good all the time; and, all the time God is good, all the time! Providence prevails and teaches. Threads and weaving of the late pastor, Father Edward Popielarz, a parish priest and professor, taught many and me, acceptance, a covenant of freedom, an agreement to set one soaring from falling to rising aiming for the moon and landing among the shining stars, at least. There, faiths, a little not a lot like that flicker of starlight, shines, sees one through ordeals and places we'd rather not go. Fr. Pops, as we called him, may have wanted to skip his alcohol attachment, to borrow Saints John of the Cross and Teresa of Avila, Spain's description, but, he embraced his whole story and learned from it. He was first to say never to reject ones story. He spread the Good News with a fresh ardor, and, an aroma and fragrance of Christ, with a new evangelizing long before it became stylish to call it new.

In the dumps of my Detroit, of Kingston, Jamaica, of Haiti, of El Salvador's barrio hospital chapel where the blood of the Salvadoran Archbishop Oscar Romero stains the marble floor at the altar where he was murdered, garden fresh tales blossom in mentors and parents, teachers and leaders who show the way.

The eight beatitudes of Matthew (Chapter 5: 1-12) are the acceptance way of life. Like my tennis shoe laces that I could only tie with one loop in kindergarten much to the chagrin and punishment of my gym teacher, who faced me in the corner toward the wall until I learned how to tie two loops, now, both loops link and are tied like the gift and grace all of life has been over time.

THREE

"Sometimes at the moment of despair a wave of light breaks
into our darkness, and it is as though a voice were saying:
"You are accepted. You are accepted, accepted by that which
is greater than you, and name of which you do not know.
Do not ask for the name now; perhaps you will find it later.
Do not try to do anything now; perhaps later you will
do much. Do not seek anything, do not intend anything.
Simply accept the fact that you are accepted." If that happens
to us, we experience grace. After such an experience...
everything is transformed. In that moment, grace conquers
sin, and reconciliation bridges the gulf of estrangement."
—Paul Tillich, The Shaking of the Foundation

I f I am afraid to be myself I will never be happy.

Happiness is the aim of healthy religion, it seems to me. Favor, grace
and blessing are like that. Fear of being myself shuts one down. He or

she freezes, even becomes numb with indifference. Life is squeezed out of one, then. The fullness of life promised by the Savior is a short-lived experience. Living organisms grow or die. My heart breaks as I watch other communities convert warehouses in galleries, cafes and worship spaces while closures of Catholic churches mount across the USA, it seems.

Community is an aspect that attracts people to each other, to churches, to growing deeper faith in small groups even out of the thousands in mega-churches today. Vatican II stressed community yet parishioners, even some pastors, leaders, may have resisted it, fear its intimate component in the exchange of a handshake before receiving Holy Communion. Liturgical renewal limps yet five decades since Vatican II. Consequently, community does also. Liturgy means "work of the people" from the Greek and, indeed that is what pastors and parishioners need to think, beyond mergers, clusters, and personnel problems that are left to Rome to settle, rather than local bishops who originally carried and led in its early days before centralization from the top began to steer while pastors bowed to the Vatican as they looked for others to imagine community and solve problems. As more and more churches are shuttered, who is leading?

Fifty years since its start in 1962, the ecumenical second Vatican Council emerges for me as one that aimed to be about 'fresh air' in a stuffy church, the reason Pope John XXIII convened the world's bishops, advisers, theologians, and more.

"In my lifetime and I think in the lifetime of most people, the full implications of this Council will not have been grasped. There is an awful lot in there that has not surfaced yet, that has not really taken hold. It is there, we know it is there because we have worked on it, we know its implications, but it has not flowered yet, it's there. I think that we don't have to go anywhere else," the late John F. Dearden, former

Archbishop of Detroit, said on March 22, 1984, at the Center for Pastoral Studies at the Orchard Lake Schools, Orchard Lake, MI.

A plan and mission was announced as it was invested in by thousands of bishops, among others at Vatican II.

The court jester comes to mind, a story I would not skip. She seemed to teach wisdom in her foolish ways. Once upon a time, the jester acted so foolishly that the King gave her his walking stick with instructions to keep it until she found a bigger fool than herself.

Time unfolded and the King grew ill. With his family, middlemen and ministers at his bedside, the King voiced: "I am going on a journey from which I will not return, so, I called you here to bid you farewell."

The jester stepped forth upon hearing these words.

"Your Majesty, when you crossed the lands and kingdoms over the seas to meet with your people, your nobles and foreign powers, your servants always went before you, making necessary preparations. May I ask what preparations Your Majesty has made for this long journey before you know?" "Alas, I have made no plans," he said with a bowed head.

Leaning over the King's bed, the jester handed the King the walking stick for she had found a bigger fool than herself.

A people without a vision and plan perish, the psalmist notes in the Good Book.

Vatican II's document on the liturgy declaring that Mass was to be in the vernacular, was a plan that was the first of these historic papers to be promulgated in that Council that met from 1962-65.

"I think that we have not yet fully realized the potential of the liturgical renewal that is called for," Dearden said twenty years after the Council's start. "Now we have people participating in the liturgy although it is not fully, actively and consciously so," he concluded. "Part of that is due to a prior problem, we have not yet developed as we would quite want to, the sense of community."

We can't skip that part. The Liturgy of the Hours needs to be implemented also. This prayer of the people at the parish level daily has been neglected.

"The pursuit of happiness is a summons of the heart to pursue the greatness of the soul," Benedictine religious, Joan Chittister, of Benetvision, a research center for contemporary spirituality in Erie, Pennsylvania, noted.

Soul work is about growing an interior life. It is.

FOUR

"I think that there are certain things that people have to
be prepared to make almost a cultural need to achieve.
And, that is community. Look how many people still
resist, looking out over the people, deep down, even the
simple action of exchanging peace among the people at
Mass. It tells you that our culture is not moved in this
direction. As a Christian people this is something. I think
that we have to face it, and, it isn't just teaching, that
you get these people to realize what we are striving for, is
something profoundly deep, and, the roots of it are within
us now, and, the light has come to us through Christ."
                        —Cardinal John F. Dearden of Detroit, Michigan
                                                    March 22, 1984

Back in 1976, altar servers were treated to a Detroit Tiger baseball game by their pastor at Saint Raymond Church in Detroit, south of Eight Mile Road, near Schoenherr. When they were finally settled in their seats to play ball, Father Terry Kerner asked for the where-abouts of one of the missing lads. "Oh, Father, Tommy's at the confession stand," shouted a classmate. How easy it is to mix up terms like concession and confession. A single letter makes all the difference for a word's meaning.

Would I skip the Detroit Tigers along with Easter? This cherished celebration of baseball by National Baseball League's A. Bartlett Giamatti, is a rite of Spring that fans wouldn't think of skipping, except if the players went on strike and didn't consider how fans would miss baseball in Motown, home of the Supremes, the professional Detroit Lions football team, the Pistons basketball team, and, the Detroit Red Wings, among other respected sport forces here.

"Sports recall the purpose of freedom every time they are enacted to show how to be free and to be complete and connected, unimpeded and integrated all at once," claims Giamatti, the former president of Yale University.

This Spring, like each year, Comerica Park will be the gathering place of countless lives longing for a pause and a "seventh inning stretch" of sorts from the hard work of the fragile game of life we play daily.

The pastoral green grass and whistling breeze will blow about some sunny stories of families and friends with lightheartedness and laughter as spectators fill the seats at the park in downtown Detroit. A pause from the delicate balance of life's challenges will have participants pondering life's meaning, and more, in between innings and outs.

Morphing, even mending will soothe weary souls some as watchers recreate and refresh for a few hours, at least. Like life, the ball is batted while fans hope for honest play by all, here, at home, in the workplace, and schools. Some elderly will settle in a seat once they've climbed the steps, and, be grateful for being there. Even alive!

Baseball's momentary escape into freedom sends one's heart chasing one's wildest dreams and daring ventures, dashing toward a finish line that inevitably meets each of us one day when passing over. For me, the thrill of high school football and basketball, taught me relished social skills and graces untaught in most homes today, sad to admit.

There's unity in great teams and households, among other systems and organizations. One, holy, catholic, and apostolic, for example are marks of the Catholic Church. Unity is created. It's worked at. Far from a given, unity is an intention of leaders from the top down. One's ego, personal gain and glory is forfeited for the greater good, the common good of the organization, philosophers remind us often. When I sense it and watch it, I stand back at its beauty. It is rare, but it is possible. As a pastor, I saw glimpses of unity especially when the pastoral workers were on the same page, of one mind, a single mission, and, a common aim. People are led to unity. A receptionist once observed: "We saw you working as hard as the rest of us at Brightmoor's Saint Christine Church, so, we followed with enthusiasm for the goals."

What kills the team spirit and aims is gossip, unhealed wounds and disagreements, a lack of prayer and connect daily with the Creator, crisp, clear, direct, and concise communications and goals, lack of investment by some co-workers, and incompetence that rides without consequences. Jesus was so good at leading, and dying, because of his time apart and away for pause and reflection. Truth, however, also has its price, as it did for him when he challenged systems and spoke truth to power.

Teamwork is similar in businesses and pastoral settings in many ways. Recreation and renewal of one's self and soul is a requirement for all players. Even in the pause of voices singing, "America the Beautiful," or, the "Star Spangled Banner," baseball has us rounding the bases of life tripping here, falling there, rising, even being caught living life less than fully. At Mass, worshippers are invited to full, active and conscious participation in the first of sixteen documents promulgated by the second Vatican Council on the liturgy. Being less that one's best in praying, singing, and participating brings down the assembly to another level. Community limps when liturgy planning lacks also.

With twenty-six letters in the alphabet, how frequently mistakes may emerge as humans strive to put on their lips the letters, words and sentences in one's mind. Communicating one's thoughts in a crisp, concise way is an arduous task for anyone, let alone young people limping along with letters to craft words and paragraphs.

Imagine comprehending God pitching his tent, as it were, among us, as the Maker established permanence and residence among us on earth. Jesus has risen and joins us at home with the hungry, the lost, estranged, naked, imprisoned and thirsty, among others. Easter could not be skipped by me. Its mighty message blesses believers with the peace of Christ in the wilderness and wonderland everywhere. Through the storms the blessing, favor and grace begs to be carried home rejoicing again and again into our own doors!

Play ball this Spring! My dad would quickly remind me, adding, "And, play well being the best player, the best priest, the best leader you can be in giving your all!" Dad worked two jobs to help make ends meet. When he took us fishing, or, up North, it was a special time to bond.

Amen.

FIVE

Climb every mountain, search high and low,
follow every byway, every path you know.
Climb every mountain, ford every stream, follow
every rainbow, till you find your dream,
A dream that will need all the love you can give,
everyday of your life for as long as you live.
Climb every mountain, ford every stream, follow
every rainbow, till you find your dream.
—Oscar Hammerstein, The Sound of Music

"The mountains skipped like rams, the hills like the lambs of the flock. Why is it O sea that you flee? O Jordan that you turn back? You mountains that you skip like rams" Psalm 114 notes in the Good Book. This song commemorates Israel's deliverance from Egypt. It is a hymn about God's choosing of Israel as his own special people. It tells a story about my older brothers and sisters in the Jewish faith tradition. They are special. The Exodus story is one of

25

deliverance, of passing over and through a Promised Land. It is also a tale of commitment and single-minded resolve led by Moses and Joshua over forty years. Oppression today behooves me to speak up when others simply sit when people are pressed and packed down, and abused. At a Vatican-hosted concert commemorating the Holocaust, Hitler's World War II effort to exterminate all Jews, in 1994, Blessed John Paul II, who attended, said: "We risk making the victims of the most atrocious deaths die again if we do not have a passion for justice."

Everyone matters. You matter. And, all others also. Foes also. Those principles are reminders to me about the dignity of all people. Even amid the violence gripping this Nation, I am called to be a peacemaker in the spirit of the Sermon on the Mount, the Beatitudes of Jesus in Matthew's Gospel, Chapter 5: 1-12.

During the Vatican Council II, the fathers spent time questioning whether Mary, holy Mother of God, would be included in the document on the Church given that she was called the "perfect disciple." In the Constitution on the Church (Lumen Gentium), Chapter Eight centers her in the middle of the writing about the Church. It is called, "The Role of the Blessed Virgin May, Mother of God, in the Mystery of Christ and the Church."

Mothers are the center of households and families. My own mother was that, and more. Moms call members of the family together. She leads in her special way, like dad's are called to provide for and protect with a quality of life and security family living needs. They are special.

"Hail, Holy Queen" is a special hymn to Mary. It reads:

Hail, Holy Queen, Mother of Mercy, our life, our sweetness, and our hope. To you do we cry, poor banished children of Eve. To you do we send up our sighs, mourning and weeping in this valley of tears.

Turn then, most gracious advocate, your eyes of mercy toward us, and after this exile show unto us the blessed fruit of thy womb, Jesus. O clement, O loving, O sweet Virgin Mary.

When these words are sung at the end of a funeral for a priest, my own mother, and, my godmother come to mind. Both were serious about their role as parent, sponsor, spouse, mother, and neighbor. From both of them I learned so much about hospitality, inclusion and compassion. With my own dad, and godfather, I learned how to work well, and fast, and, how to pause from time to time. After all, dad would say: "You think too much!" Upon hearing that clarion call, it was time to play once more.

SIX

They called the church together and reported
what God had done with them and how God
opened the door of faith to the Gentiles.

Acts 14:27

The mystic and bold reformer, Saint Catherine of Siena, notes: "The Devil will take advantage of your blindness and put before you a banquet of his delights, colored to look like something that is good for you." She viewed life as a dialog between God and us, something I never want to skip. Perhaps Easter gets skipped this year, but, not my daily connection and conversation with God.

How important communication with God is always. Like the collaboration and subsidiarity that Vatican II urged, this divine connection is vital for the ardor and enthusiasm that "good news" instills. Take, for example, any mother with a child in her womb. My mother and dad's two sets of twins plus three more children on the way was always good news. Deep joy marked mom's pregnancies. And, although she also spoke of the terrible pain involved in moving life through the birth canal, delight spread across her face as she told me about the birth of my twin sister, Patti and me.

Ash Wednesday begins Lent (from the Old English, "Lencten," meaning, springtime) on February 13, 2013. The season excites me about the possibilities and opportunities for morphing, mending, and, inviting God to make me a new creation these forty days of this campaign of Christian service. Lent reminds me of the words of Blessed Teresa of Calcutta: "The fruit of silence is prayer; the fruit of prayer is faith; the fruit of faith is love; the fruit of love is service; the fruit of service is peace," words that were cited by Pope John Paul II, October 20, 2003.

And, I want to skip Easter and go to Easter Island, a remote and mysterious wasteland discovered by a Dutch exploration on Easter Sunday in 1722? Authors Terry Hunt and Carl Lipo unravel the island's intrigue in The Statues That Walked. Let me check if I have enough money to purchase the airline ticket now to take me there, that site near Chile.

Even as Teresa's words emerge as I think of Easter and all that leads up to its real meaning beyond jelly beans, bunnies and butter lambs, those of Bishop Kenneth Untener on ministry, mark me for this Lenten season:

"It helps now and then, to step back and take a long view. The Kingdom of God is not only beyond our efforts, it is even beyond our vision.

We accomplish in our lifetime only a tiny fraction of the magnificent enterprise that is God's work. Nothing we do is complete, which is a way of saying that the Kingdom always lies beyond us. No statement says all that could be said. No prayer fully expresses our faith. No confession brings perfection. No pastoral visit brings wholeness. No program accomplishes the Church's mission. No set of goals and objectives includes everything.

This is what we are about: We plant the seeds that one day will grow. We water seeds already planted, knowing that they hold future promise.

We lay foundations that will need further development. We provide yeast that produces effects far beyond our capabilities.

We cannot do everything, and there is a sense of liberation in realizing that. This enables us to do something, and to do it very well. It may be incomplete, but it is a beginning, a step along the way, an opportunity for the Lord's grace to enter and do the rest. We may never see the end results, but that is the difference between the master builder and the worker.

We are workers, not master builders; ministers not messiahs. We are prophets of a future not our own."

Prayer, fasting and alms giving, the pillars of this trek through the solemn and glorious celebration of Mass on Holy Thursday when the penitential season of Lent ends, and, the Triduum makes its debut, including Good Friday, Holy Saturday's Vigil and Easter Sunday. Bells chime out with the sung Gloria, light floods the edifice, and, as the late, and enthusiastic Untener, a native of Detroit who grew up near the historic Belle Isle on the Detroit River, and, longtime bishop of Saginaw, Michigan, says, the great three days begin "when we wrestle with the great questions -- your great questions. Come and join us as we pray together with the Lord who addressed the problem of evil and put his own life on the line for our sake. This is not past history. This is our story," urged Untener, who worried that "we're losing the Triduum."

Famous worldwide for his vest pocket, checkbook-size Little Books on Lent, Easter, Stewardship, and more, I looked forward to conversations with the lively Untener who instilled fervor and motivation into preachers. He required his priests to join in workshops with Cathy Haven, a former Michigan Catholic reporter, and himself to craft effective and brief homilies. The pastoral leader wanted his clergy to be pastors beyond CEOs or administrators. He urged parishes one Lent to think about the actions that they determine, and, their effect on the poor in the Saginaw, MI., diocese he led for decades before his death at 66. Liturgy was more important for pastors and parishioners than administration that others could do. Preaching better, and, praying a meaningful Mass was emphasized over all the other distractions in parish life that take people from their primary mission as church.

And, I want to skip this Easter? Go figure. Why?

Sure, I was sick and was in bed all day with that horrific flu epidemic this past Christmas Day after presiding at Mass in St. Thecla Church in Clinton Township, and, at Our Lady Queen of Apostles Church in Hamtramck, Michigan. True, I missed my family's Christmas Day dinner in Romeo. Of course, idolizing one day to be the picture-perfect photo together is not what Christmas is about amid the hassles, shopping, baking, and high expectations people put on one another. But, so did Bruce, my sister, Marcyanna's husband, have the flu also. My siblings stayed for a bit and left since he was in bed sick. But, skipping Easter over all this? I don't know.

That's another story.

SEVEN

Remember, you are dust and into dust you will return!
–Words said while ashes in the form of a cross were
pressed on my forehead on Ash Wednesday, the
start of Lent's penitential season of 40 days

R epent and believe in the Gospel.

Those words also accompanied the dark, shiny black ashes, remains from the burnt palm fronds reminiscent of the crowds in Jerusalem hailing Jesus as he rode into town on a donkey. Both options were up to the priest to say as he administered ashes at our Romanesque edifice built in 1927 at Townsend and Miller in Detroit. And, days later, Jesus is crucified on a cross on Mount Calvary amid two thieves. Cruel, I thought. One of them, Dismas, wins heaven on his 'death bed' cross after Jesus assures him of Paradise. When I think of Jesus' execution I think of man and women's inhumanity toward each other. The other night, for example, after paying my respects to the late Bishop Moses

Anderson, the first African-American bishop in Detroit, in the Most Blessed Sacrament Cathedral on Woodward near Davison, Dennis asked to be dropped off at a favorite coney shop south of the Mother Church of the Archdiocese of Detroit. While we emerged from the car, multiple shots rang out. They got our attention.

Violence is as common as blowing one's nose it seems in my good ole USA. Daily reports of deaths in Detroit worry many of us. The gun debate heightens, and, people seem to be getting armed with these weapons of mass destruction as massacres mount in this country also. Sad times. And, I want to skip Easter? How would I wrestle with the mysteries of suffering, dying, rising, and, the entire paschal mystery of Jesus' own death and triumph on Easter Sunday. O death where is your sting, where is your victory. Good prevails in the end. Witnessing the cycle of violence, however, and the disrespect for life in and outside the womb worries me.

Furthermore, this saga of sadness seems to be the new normal while people sit and refuse to speak up against the arsenal of deadly tools. Those who live by the sword die by it, I recall paraphrasing Jesus' warning. A recent meeting proposed that a step-by-step plan be hatched to mentor children and parents in the law of love and the commandments listed in Deuteronomy, and Exodus, in the Good Book, once more. After all, Seneca, the philosopher, said, reminders are more important than new information. My Motown needs to mount an offensive to strengthen family. While my siblings and I were raised in Detroit, our doors at home could be left open when we went off to do errands. Today, large parcels of land are empty of any houses. Tall weeds hide some of the homes remaining in Detroit's population of less than that of Milwaukee. It's an agony in the garden. It's our own string of more than fourteen traditions, stations of the cross of Jesus depicting brutal cruelty and a culture of death. Too much. Breaks my heart to hear of drive-by shootings of babies in homes, and more, daily. To think of crimes that don't get reported, or heard on line, TV and radio. Scary! Time for prayer and fasting, lone remedies to restore evergreen hope, and, other virtues of faith, charity, prudence, justice, temperance, and fortitude, classic strengths that need to be reinforced once more. Additional deadly sins have been added to the traditional list by the pope.

Our own family procession to church on Easter Sunday was a parade of color in itself. Nine of us in single file with dad in the lead with his fast feet. Mom watched for the smallest feet at the tail of the long line off to Saint Thomas the Apostle Church, miles from our home near the Detroit City Airport near Connor and French Road, not far from Holy Name of Jesus Church on McNichols and Van Dyke. I'd go there for confession. I forget which priest was kinder there but he had a reputation for brief encounters in reconciliation when I confessed my sins there. Like clockwork routine, we went monthly to the sacrament of penance, also called confession or reconciliation. In this dark, tiny cubicle, I'd tick off my litany list of missing the mark, "of harmatia," sin. When I was in the second grade, in fact, the sisters of Saint Joseph of the third order of Saint Francis of Garfield Heights, OH., trained us to know what comprises sin - to know it's wrong, to intend to do the violation of God's laws, and to commit the act. It was difficult for me to search my heart. I did, however. It was frightening to tell the confessor my sins. Burden was lifted, nevertheless, and, a relationship was restored, praise God. Then, I'd try to do better. Would fail and fall, repeat sins, but work at them. Had to, or else. That's how we were taught in the 50s. Today, what is taught, more importantly, whose example shines through adults, parents, systems, authority?

After all, religion is caught more than taught. Use words only when necessary, Saint Francis of Assisi taught, suggesting that our lives be used to show forth acts of kindness and love.

Wow!

I'll miss much if I skip Easter, no?

EIGHT

Our eyes were opened to the enormity of the problem
of missing and exploited children. As the parents of
the murdered teenager, Molly Bish, we learned that
teen-age girls are at a higher risk for non-family, or, so
called, "stranger" abductions, than younger children.
We all bear mutual responsibility for our children
because they are so trusting. If we all do something,
anything, our children, our families will be safer.
  –John Bish, with his wife, Magi, of West Warren, MA.,
and Class of '71 St. Mary's College, Orchard Lake, MI.

The lovely, engaging Molly Bish never returned from her lifeguard shift in 2000. Unsolved mystery, among others that leave investigators, among others, baffled forever.

Like the mystery, misery, and more, of the agony in the garden for Jesus and his companions, we long to know more. Yet, good triumphing over evil, may suffice, for some. Molly's parents are horrified, and, their lives were morphed forever at her disappearance over a dozen years ago. Things, relationships, and life changed after Molly's demise.

"To accept is to live and let live with those realities you cannot change, but, in the meantime, busy yourself changing those realities you can change," noted the late Father Edward D. Popielarz, a pastor and professor at the Orchard Lake Schools for half of his vocation, while his remaining years on earth were spent as a pastor at Shrine of St. Joseph Church in Pontiac, close enough for my classmates and me to attend his famously helpful class in acceptance Tuesdays after 7 pm Mass in the lower level of the quaint church.

Add to that the virtues, the inner strengths of courage, wisdom, and zeal of the prolific writer and distinguished Catholic preacher, the blessed, Bishop Fulton Sheen, who said:

"Jews, Protestants, and Catholics should unite against a common foe. It is not a unity of religion we plead for -- that is impossible when purchased at the cost of the unity of truth -- but a unity of religious people...In a word, if anti-Christ has his fellow-travelers, we may not be able to meet in the same pew --would to God we did -- but we can meet on our knees."

We can.

Connoisseurs of faith, like that of experienced tasters of Merlot or Shiraz, get down into the details of the grapes, the gardens they're grown in, the state, and, chilling white, while serving red wine at room temperature. Even faith traditions get comfortable with their own. And, silos are erected and territory protected, at least, about doctrine and dogma. Yet, love, charity, and other virtues and strengths move beyond walls encircling camps, crusades, causes and particular persuasions of belief.

These unsolved mysteries can be settled, prevented in the first place if neighbors became what Jesus invited when he said "to love your neighbor as yourself." It would seem that we love self little since one can avoid others nearby, and, even regularly escape anonymously by driving from one's attached garage without ever knowing one's next door resident. Once, I asked a leading Vatican official to give a talk on "love of God and neighbor," and the retired prelate asked, "Larry, why would you want to do that?" "Because we don't know our neighbors," I shot back quickly. "Well...I don't know my neighbors," he confessed. A culture of anonymity these days would alarm my parents.

So much mystery in failing to know each other, to know a neighbor, or, his or her family, their story, struggles, and then some. Yet, a mounting offensive to get neighbors to take time to know each other is part of the Inclusive Communities Uniting, in St. Clair Shores, among other cities in metropolitan Detroit.

How often at funerals I hear the faithful say that they didn't know that the deceased was ill. Talking, calling, contacting and communicating with others works to grow trust.

More mystery.

Taking time to tell tales is key to building community. In the neighborhood I grew up in, we knew the neighborhood nurse, Mrs. Lewandowski, our next door neighbor, Mr. Kowalski, Josie and Ed Stepowski and Family, the John, Brenda and Paul Domenick household, Raymond Malinowski, and, his parents, and, our cousins, Betty, Tom, Marie, and Pete, dad's brother's children of Uncle Pete and Rose Ventline, who also lived on Arcola Street where my family resided until the civil unrest and rioting moved my parents to Warren where security, and, a quality of life is a priority for Mayor Jim Fouts.

After World War II, perhaps amid the military industrial complex that President Dwight Eisenhower warned against, community began to fade, like front porches and free-standing garages. Neighborliness limps now. And, criminal behavior is harder to detect because of that. Things, toys, boats and more seem more important than people. Second graders have all the tech toys to keep them locked into the Internet, I-pad, I-pod, TV, and such. One wonders what God thinks when rapport with such things trumps relationships with parents, siblings, and kids in the neighborhood. Reaching low to pick up, to lift life, and, to serve, is a hallmark of the Christian life. In fact, Catholics have an entire body of social thought that urges believers to speak up for others, for workers, for the most vulnerable in or outside the womb, on the battlefield, in the neighborhood, and, at school and in the home, the domestic church, for sure. Churches grow relationships and community in small groups, even among mega-churches that thrive these days while some observers wonder, asking, "Is that church?" It seems that bringing people together to care and be compassionate qualifies even where "two or more are gathered in my name," said Jesus.

Father, forgive me, for I have sinned. And, nudge me to wake up, speak up, and be charitable.

And, I want to skip Easter with so much pain? How will I find time? Hmm.....we'll see!

NINE

At the cross her stations keeping stood
the mournful mother weeping.
—Words of an ancient, Lenten hymn
about Mary

While driving through the Detroit/Windsor tunnel, I think about grief and loss, at times. And, once I thought of Mary Chapin's 2012 album, "Ashes and Roses." With heartaches by the number, divorce, the loss of a parent, and a serious illness confronted her. She processed her desolation and loss of life, love and more, by way of songs. Medical mysteries and miracles, including visions of heaven by a neuro-surgeon, Dr. Alexander interviewed on TV, for example, his Proof of Heaven, confirms that healing, mending, even resurrected living, and beyond, is real. Easter life and the 50-day season through Pentecost Sunday is like that! Flowers, butterflies and a flooded, radiant -lighting experience for this one physician, among others, for example, concludes the coming together of what scientists and faiths have been

41

exploring for centuries. Psychiatry and spirituality are more than talking now given that they have come of age!

Like the intimates of Jesus during his hours of death, and, at the last supper with his closest disciples, grief is that normal and natural process that one experiences and feels to get to the other side, to the light, to healing, mending and recovery. Unless feelings of loss are felt, they drop into depression, swallowed grief that shows its ugly head years later, when one wonders why now?

Feelings, like anger, must have flooded people during the life and trials of Jesus in Jerusalem. Anger is real, even deadly. It harms one's being and body each time one erupts with it. A chemical in one's body is released with anger. That can be harmful to one's heart's wellness. Storing angry feelings within one's self will cause havoc within one's temple of the Holy Spirit.

Anger is like that. It is a sin in my faith tradition as a Catholic, even though St. Paul, notes in Ephesians, "to be angry but don't let the sun set on it." A palm-size booklet, I wrote, says it well in, Anger: Reminders for Raging Times. It's a handbook to use before anger or rage flare. It merits keeping nearby to remind self and others of what one already may know, but may forget when angry and reacting to situations at home or work, for example.

Anger lurks when one thinks she or he is being treated unjustly. Feelings like mad, sad, glad, or scared help to cope. No one can make one angry. One chooses to be angry or enraged. Walk away, run away, exercise away your stress and anger daily for about an hour of recreation, down time, meditation, or, being quiet before the Blessed Sacrament. Rosary beads also help one calm down by repetitive prayers. Google the word, rosary, to learn how to say it by yourself, or with others.

One can step aside and take a deep breath when anger looms large.

Tell the person you're angry with that you need to cool off, but, do decide a time to meet later.

Express anger in appropriate, nonviolent ways.

Recalling that conflict may be normal but violence is not, even though it seems today that violence is as common as blowing one's nose.

Getting enraged doesn't help anyone, most of all, one's self. When angry, naming the problem that makes one upset helps, and, claiming the issue as one's own is key to resolution to it. Only then, can one tame the helpful way to handle or manage the issue.

One has to own his or her angry feelings. When young, one may have been told to stuff your anger. "Boys won't like girls who get angry," one may have been told. Unlearn that. Boys may have been told that men don't cry. Unlearn that. Honor feelings and feel them.

It's how one expresses the feelings that may endanger others.

No one is perfect, and, everyone is incomplete and capable of falling short of ideals. Put yourself in another's shoes. Get help if anger is out of control in your life, or, if it has become a habit.

Unresolved anger could become resentment and cynicism. That's like drinking poison intended for someone else!

And, ask God to assist you in letting go of angry feelings.

In the sermon on the Mount, Jesus says, "You shall not kill," and, adds to it the proscription of anger, hatred and vengeance. (Matthew 5:21)

Skip anger. It's not worth it.

TEN

You have to be taught to love. The family is nothing
but love and love is giving oneself to the well being
of all. It is working for common happiness.
- Archbishop Oscar Romero of San Salvador

You do. You have to be carefully taught. Examples showcase love.
They do. Children love to watch mom and dad live out their love
at home. And, they are happier also because of this experience. They
live what they learn from dad and mom. They do.

Marriage is tough. It does require time to work at building a relationship
beyond rapport alone. In the living out of matrimony, conflicts arise,
differences emerge, and family cohesion is threatened. Nipping the issue
in the bud soon after it happens helps. Marriage involves the suffering,
dying and rising entailed in the spiritual walk and trek through life.
Accepting that reality merits attention. Perfect marriages may be made
in heaven but on earth, they're a struggle, but, worth it.

All the years that I've worked with Retrouvaille, and, Marriage Encounter, including Bethany, an organization for divorces and separated Catholics in Detroit, I've learned to grow with couples in their own commitment. Priests write talks to present right along with mentor couples who share on various topics that are helpful to participants in the weekend encounter.

Like faith, marriage and family, is a journey. Singles and pastors are called to the same chaste living of faithfulness. Life is a journey like that of Jesus' life.

In the Footsteps of Jesus: A Chronicle of His Life and the Origins of Christianity, by Jean-Pierre Isbouts (National Geographic Books, 2012), the way of the cross is pictured.

This thick and beautiful tome returns me to my first Holy Land pilgrimage in the '80s with a rabbi and a pastor who led me into the heart and soul of Jesus's earthly life once more. A virtual trip that enriched my faith, the 368-page book will edify even the pilgrim who has not been there yet.

The author has written widely on the genesis of Judaism, Christianity, and Islam. With maps, graphs, archaeological artifacts, and photos in hand and word intended to reconstruct the social, cultural, and historical milieu of the rise of Jesus, he leads through the ancient land of the Roman Empire prior to Jesus' debut. I was moved by his text challenging me more deeply to follow the Way, Truth and Life.

I felt that I was following Jesus again as I journey into Capernaum, Galiee, Tyre and Sidon, and the Decapolis before the final entry of Jesus in Jerusalem, where Isbouts paints an elaborate reconstruction of the Passion story. Final parts of the tome trace the Easter story with Jewish

Christians in Judea and Jerusalem along with gentiles in Greece, Asia Minor, and Syria up to the early Roman Empire.

It arrived in time for Easter. A graceful gift.

I better skip skipping Easter this year.

I will.

ELEVEN

Great souls die and our reality, bound to them,
takes leave of us. Our souls, dependent upon
their nurture, now shrink, wizened. Our minds,
formed and informed by their radiance, fall away...

...And when great souls die, after a period peace
blooms, slowly and always irregularly...
Our sense restored, never to be the same,
whisper to us. They existed. They existed.
We can be. Be and be better.
For they existed.

–Maya Angelou

46 million people in poverty is unacceptable.
–http://www.catholiccharitiesusa.org/

When I was very young, I remember skipping to, "Lou, Lou, skip to my Lou, Skip to my Lou, my darling! Fly's in the buttermilk, Shoo, fly, shoo, skip to my Lou, my darling! Lost my partner, what'll I do, skip to my Lou, my darling! I'll find another one, prettier too, skip to my Lou, my darling! I've got a friend his name is Bill, he used to have a house on the side of a hill, One leg's longer than the other one still. Skip to my Lou, my darling."

It was a song I sang with spontaneity and joy. I just remember the tune, the beat and my twin sister and I, skipping to the sound of the words. It's just one of those things that is etched forever on one's heart. Joy is like that, also.

"I bring you news of great joy, a joy to be shared by the whole people." (Luke 2:10)

"How I rejoiced when they said to me, 'Let us go to the house of Yahweh! (Psalms 122)

Other hymns, especially songs of Lent and Easter, resound within me, including, "Crown Him with Many Crowns," "Faith of Our Fathers!," "Lift High the Cross," "Amazing Grace," "O Happy Day," "Silent Night," "Joy to the World," "Hail, Holy Queen," "Ashes," "Come, Holy Ghost," "The Old Rugged Cross," "Veni Sancte Spiritu," "O Happy Day," "Ave Maria," "Climb Every Mountain," "A Mighty Fortress Is Our God," and the Polish, "Sto Lat," ("May you live 100 years!"), and, "I Will Raise You Up," among so many more Easter season hymns for fifty days. Music ministry is like that. It penetrates my heart and soul. It makes me want to fully, actively and consciously participate at Mass, as urged by Vatican II. After a funeral at Sacred Heart Church, in Roseville, MI., Deacon Paul Lippard and Father Gene Katcher led the singing of "Happy Birthday," before the funeral luncheon. I took notice. How fitting. New life is like that. Welcome Easter life! A passing over into the eternal lap of the Maker. What joy that must be for the deceased who morphs into more like the physicists who claim that matter and energy are not destroyed but changed. Consequently the matter of my body is not destroyed at death but morphs, and becomes more.

Festivity is like that also. It affirms my "yes" to life, to Easter, to more! Mozart's music moves me also. Forty days of Lent, the Triduum of Holy Thursday, Good Friday, the Easter Vigil and Easter Sunday, and, fifty days diving into reflecting on the Paschal Mystery, of suffering, dying, and rising. Fifty days from Easter Sunday to Pentecost help me to wrestle in my heart with its own weather, wonder, and works in praise of our Easter life. They are really one "great Sunday" celebrated in joyful exultation, as Saint Athanasius noted.

A double alleluia is added to the dismissal at Mass, morning prayer and vespers, and throughout the octave of the first eight days of the Easter season. Talk about a full plate to digest, enjoy, savor and relish long.

Not to mention the huge paschal candle skyrocketing into the sky of the edifice, a symbol of the presence of the risen Christ among the people of God.

Easter baptisms flood with joy the families of the infants who are baptized these Sundays following the rite of Christian initiation of adults at the Easter Vigil when heart and soul chimes and rings out others who join the family, even partake of the sacraments of initiation of baptism, Eucharist and confirmation. The heartache that is part of life has me recalling how to assist children and others about the escalating violence surrounding us all in this culture today. As the prophet, Isaiah sings, "Comfort, Give Comfort. . .," listening and consoling may well be the role of parents and catechists, among others. Grandparents also can help assure youngsters after the Newtown, Connecticut school massacre after six and seven-year-old students, their principal, and other adults were shot down early in the morning after classes started. Primary formators in the faith are parents, yet, it does take a village to supplant the primary role of parents as educators and models of faith for the family. Parents cannot be replaced. Strengthening family is building the foundation of our society, the domestic church at home.

Answers to students about incidents where students no longer show up for school, given the horror of Newtown, for example, need to be brief, specific, and age appropriate. The aim is to make them aware, not to scare! "A bad thing happened to them. But, mom and dad, your teachers and others will be here for you, and, will protect you," is a way to respond to a curious, grieving child. Elders are wise and helpful. Reassure youth. Hold them in evergreen hope. Swoop them up into your arms. Tell them, "I love you!"

The mystery of death, like that of the agony in the garden, and beyond, to Calvary, takes time to process, to grieve. Dreams and nightmares may accompany a child's sleeping hours. Observing them during the days after a trauma is important in the healing process. Assure them that things will be OK, not to worry. "Grieve, but do not grieve as those without hope," the Good Book notes in the First Letter of John. Managing stress, grief, loss, even anger as soon as possible after a traumatic event will do a world of good in staving off counseling later in the child's life. After all, swallowing one's grief without dealing with it, becomes depression later in his or her life. "Let the children come to me," Jesus said in the Good Book. Doing that will allow children to be free to ask about the demise of other children caught in the line of fire and bullets, or, tragedy.

A Chinese proverb sums up ways to family and world peace:

"If there is righteousness in the heart,
there will be beauty in the character.
If there is beauty in the character,

there will be love in the home.
If there is love in the home,
there will be order in the nation.
If there is order in the nation,
there will be peace in the world."

When this culture can't stay and commit long to much other than fifteen minutes of fame, as Andy Warhol once quipped, we're asked to celebrate the Christmas season beyond the day, the "to do," the twenty-four hour feast of the Nativity, well into January's Epiphany, and more. A microwave and quick, fast culture can't wait much, is impatient, and seems to get a "buzz" from speeding, and, a "I'm so busy" attitude that would cause my parents to wonder how they did it with two sets of twins when diapers were cloth, and they never seemed to tell me, "I'm too busy!" Speed, fast and quick, are the new addiction and attachment disorder, it seems to me. It will kill the soul of this nation unless we slow down, pause, reflect, and go deeper than a superfluous, cosmetic, primping the outer self without growing and attending daily to an inner life.

Even more days to fully celebrate when it comes to the Easter season, is the order of the day prescribed by the Church. After all, this is huge, Easter looms large with life, with love, even laughter and joy swells my heart with the distinguishing marks of a Christian: tranquility, humility, and, a detachment from possessing it so much that my attachment may have Saints John of the Cross or Teresa of Avila, Spain, mystics, those head over heel in love with God, cautioning me to "let go." Lighten the grip some like a golfer must, I'm told. A boldly sung -- Alleluia! -- repeated, swells the soul's celebration and season, praise the Creator.

I can't skip Easter. Football practice in high school I skipped so I could help earn some cash for our family of nine. I got in trouble, however, with the coach who banged my helmet with Bob Smith's when we were back on the field to practice for the opening game. No way. To have explored these times was to embark on a journey that runs deep in the profound mysteries of renewed and fresh living always.

So, I'll just skip skipping Easter! "Skip, skip, skip to my Lou. . .!"

TWELVE

Ring the bells that still can ring. Forget your
perfect offering. There is a crack in everything.
That's how the light gets in.

–Leonard Cohen

L ike light, the joy of a second chance, is welcoming. "Love is an endless act of forgiveness, a tender look which becomes a habit," said Peter Ustinov. Messing up is part of life. Making less than noble, loving choices, happens often. Yet, virtues, and the development of inner strengths can replace vices, or, bad habits of sin, of missing the mark.

When the Rite of Christian Initiation of Adults (RCIA) is in full swing, and, implemented as instructions and rubric rules requires the entire parish community and family forges forth in this process and procession from Ashes to Easter to Pentecost reflections of fifty days. At St. Rene Goupil in Sterling Heights, and St. Anne in Warren, MI.,

Father George Charnley, a sports enthusiast and basketball coach, used metaphors that would inspire RCIA participants to embrace the three movements of the spiritual life:

Uncovering/purgative, discovering/illuminata, and recovery/divina unitiva. From crawling to walking to running into the trusting arms of the Beloved in one's faith trek -- that's the aim toward holiness and wholeness God desires, it seems to me.

With crowds of participants in the RCIA, along with an experience of Jesus, personal prayer, and lessons from the Sunday Scriptures, humor helped to form and inform candidates for the faith journey, baptism, and reception into the Church at the Easter Vigil when dark covered the earth, and the new Light exploded with radiance everywhere from the Paschal Candle's symbol of suffering, dying and rising in Christ, the Victor who triumphed over death, once for all! Never have I witnessed such joy in the participants and their families who attended the weekly sessions. Like a Mass honoring women on Assumption eve, for the feast of Mary, Aug. 15, the wide smiles that broke forth in the women and men in line for Holy Communion, was astounding, and, had me take notice, what spirituality is all about -- awakening, attuning to, attending to, being alert to him or her in your presence at any given moment. Talk about union and communion with God! Grace does build upon human nature and experience as the Jesuit theologian, Father Karl Rahner, notes.

From the revised Roman Missal's current focus on Ash Wednesday to "begin with holy fasting this campaign of Christian service," with the organ keyboard and other musical instruments only to be used if necessary to support the assembly's singing, all the way to the exception with the joy-filled Laetare, the Fourth Sunday of Lent, right up to the Easter Vigil and Sunday Mass, the forty days, the ashes, the rich symbols of fresh fire, new water, and the fresh Word of the Exodus story up to the Gospel that tells of the stone at the tomb being removed, along with the body of Jesus, to the fresh-baked bread, and wine, movement from ashes to Easter to Pentecost, is one of a pilgrim's trek from bondage to freedom, from sin to liberation, from darkness into the Light! Awesome!

Imagine the fans, the thrill at football games of the Detroit Lions, for example. Or, how faith and family came before football for the parents of Danny Wuerffel, the quarterback who won the Heisman trophy and led his University of Florida Gators to a national championship. And, how later, he influenced quarterback, Tim Tebow, as he kneels and models faith, family and football in stadiums across the nation. As the retired pastor, and St. Gregory Parish, player, George Charnley, said, when he coached grade school basketball, "Prayer was always part of our games before and after."

The prolific writer, C.S. Lewis, in reasoning about Christianity, said, that if false, it is of no importance, and if true, of infinite importance. "The only thing it cannot be is moderately important," warned Lewis. Full, active, and conscious participation at liturgy, at life, and, in faith hope, and love. Imagining that --heaven -- and heading there to score everlasting life.

Come and see! Those words of Jesus in the Gospel are his response to those who asked where he lives. Like the Triduum days of Holy Week, we come and see. Jesus lives in the mysteries of these most holy days, the most important days of the church calendar. The mysteries, even misery of these days, and, their eventual victory over death bring up Dulcinea who morphed from Aldonza in "Man From La Mancha." She shouts out in desperation to Don Quixote, on his own death bed: "You must remember the dream...to dream the impossible dream, to fight the unbeatable foe, to bear unbearable sorrow..." Quixote was there for Aldonza/Ducinea who morphed and mended in the mystery and misery of her own story's trek through time. In turn, she was there for him as he lay passing over into glorious new life. For Christ's sake, remember.

The Catholic Guide to Depression: How the Saints, the Sacraments, and Psychiatry Help You Break Its Grip and Find Happiness Again, by Dr. Aaron Kheriaty, MD., and Monsignor John Cihak, STD, offers hope amid misery and mystery of illness. Both authors offer faithful wisdom and learned guidance in dealing with depression and anxiety. It deals with this grave and sometimes deadly affliction faced by millions. Help is on the way like Easter hope in this handbook for healing. Waiting too long prolongs depressions grip and robs one of the abundant life of the Risen Lord. Psalm 103, "The Lord is Kind and Merciful," resounds within me. Like the Passion/Palm Sunday procession of the entry into Jerusalem, the passion proclaimed in the Good Book, and, the Eucharist, this journey merits full participation this Holy Week in the services of the Triduum especially. They are a school of faith for family unmatched anywhere else in life. They are! Faithful crawl to the feasts! Hosanna to the King of Glory.

Were you there? Were you there when the held the wood of the cross and the sacred head surrounded with crowns of piercing thorns? Did On Eagle's Wings, the Seven Last Words, and, My God, My God, Why Have You Forsaken Me, shake your inner life? Were you beneath the cross adoring the crucified and victorious One?

Did the blazing fire at the Easter Vigil that shines in the darkness, in the parish parking lot, get your attention before the procession into the edifice for the Easter story's glory as it grips me? Did you come to the fresh waters of baptism and make your renewal of promises to live in the Lord's life recalling that the strife is over, the battle done now, Lent finished at Holy Thursday night's Mass?

Jesus Christ is Risen Today! At the Lamb's High Feast. "Sing me a lullaby, a love song, a requiem, Love me, comfort me, bring me to God," sings Jane Griner among the many joy-filled ministers of music this day who rock the people of God this Easter, and every Sunday that is Easter! This is the day the Lord has made, let us rejoice and be glad in it for worthy is the Lamb. Like other lambs of God who were here last Easter but gone this year.

Forty-four years ago is a long time to remember him this Memorial Day, this Easter Sunday. I was in college at St. Mary's, Orchard Lake, MI. I feared the worse when an emergency call came. I knew my brother, Lucas, was killed in Vietnam. It was February 18, 1968.

When the Vietnam Wall was erected, parishioners at St. Christine Church in Brighmoor, on Detroit's northwest side, urged me to go to Washington, D.C. There in the National Cathedral I would say out loud my brother's name amid the litany of others that fill the black granite and wet wall that challenged me to find in the heavy rain that murky and mysterious evening. I moved my finger over all the sacred names in this sacred shrine, on this holy ground, and, blessed them as they blessed me in silence that spoke a thousand words.

For three days, like that of Jesus' own Triduum of Holy Thursday, Good Friday, and the Ester Vigil/Easter Sunday, the vigil began on Veteran's Day and continued like a procession completing the reading of the holy names out loud. Tears trickled.

Other times I returned to the Vietnam Veterans Memorial in Constitution Garden, and, to Mt. Olivet Cemetery on McNichols and Van Dyke where my brother, Lucas, is buried with my parents.

Viewing Luke's name brought to mind the Tennyson poem, "The Charge of the Light Brigade": "There's not to make reply, there's not to reason why, theirs but to do and die."

Rain continued to pour down that night in D.C. The ravages of war speak volumes from the Wall. Anger and trauma still show up in the cancer from Agent Orange in so many vets now gone.

The dead deserve to be at peace. The loss in the hole in one's soul grows small as I remember my oldest brother, and all the vets at the John Dingell Veterans Hospital in downtown Detroit. In the faces of those men and women, my brother rises.

With a geranium, a crucifix, and, a red, white and blue flag this Easter Day, quietly, I'll genuflect and bow at Luke's grave this Easter, saying:

"Eternal rest grant unto them, O Lord, and let perpetual light shine upon them. May they rest in peace."

And, for those in and outside the womb, I'll say a prayer for this eternal march for life that turned forty this year. Abortion-rights activists won an epic victory four decades ago with Roe v. Wade, but, as reports and statistics show, they've been losing ever since.

Guttmacher notes a steady drop in the overall abortion rate to about 20 per 1,000 in 2008, from 30 per 1,000 mothers with a baby in their womb from ages 15 to 44 in 1981. Fewer physicians seem willing to cause more harm these days, it seems. Most Americans vote for restricting that horrific and deadly procedure these days. It seems to me that no one wants to ever need such surgery. Is one "pro-choice" to decide on wearing car seat belts? A clear and consistent ethic of life is embraced by the Catholic Church. In 1989 and 1998 the New York Times showed a shift from general acceptance of legalized abortion in the US.

God is the source of life, of risen life. Respect for life is a seamless garment, someone once said. Actions beyond words work best. I enjoy putting my arms around someone who is thinking about abortion, and announcing that I'm willing to help her, and the impregnating father be a friend of life.

Since 1973, millions of friends of life have gathered in the nation's capital to witness to Easter life. That's commendable and historic in this battle against a violent culture. One day we will win for life. However, this long, painful journey will require long-suffering and persistence. This examination of conscience for life merits the thoughtful mind of all who support life in and outside the womb. Easter is like that. It's the long journey home from ashes to Easter, from the cross to the crown.

And, to think that I even thought about skipping Easter. Shame on me.

SKIPPING EASTER

Just skip it, will you?
The Lord is my light and my salvation, whom should I fear?
The Lord is my life's refuge, of whom should I be afraid?

—Psalm 27

P lay ball!

I may be found at a baseball game at Comerica Park in downtown Detroit watching the Tigers, or, less, at Ford Field engaging in a Detroit Lions game. In high school, I joined teams to feel included and accepted, although I was not an accomplished athlete. Though I excelled academically, and, felt strange being the lone guy on the National Honor Society, being popular meant playing sports. I jumped in. There also I learn a lot about life.

In the game of life, one wins some, and, loses some. One may be excluded to play on the school sports team, or, one may be rejected by a first love, she or he may be passed over for a promotion, one gets ill, doesn't get everything she or he wants in life, and, will die one day.

Victory goes to the enduring, the long-suffering, the patient, and, virtuous who are equipped with motivation and strengths of hope, charity, prudence, fortitude, justice, faith, and temperance.

When left untaught, those mysteries of life, may have one reacting in rage to what he or she doesn't get at any given point in life. Tragically, if young people are not taught by the example of parents, among others, these mysteries of life, then violence may become the determined decision, for some, sad to admit. We witnessed this in the Newtown, CT., massacre, among other escalating rampages across the US.

Lent, and its forty day trek through Easter Sunday's fifty-day season through Pentecost, provides an opportunity to fully enter into the wrestling of these mysteries within one's center, one's soul. With the passion and victory of Christ, the arduous trek becomes good news for active participants in the Triduum of Holy Week, the three days culminating from the cross to the crown.

Skip, skipping Easter. Bring on the jelly beans, bunnies, butter lamb, ham, kielbasa, and colorfully, dyed eggs. Get the Easter basket full of food blessed. I can't wait!

It's not worth skipping. I'd miss too much.

It's too big, too huge, and, to bold to skip.

Happy Easter!

Like professional ballplayers, teams win some and lose some games.

Skipping Easter wasn't all that it looked like originally as I explored the richness of the season. Once again, I proved myself wrong. I'll be home for the holy day.

Easter Island will wait.

+

Lawrence M. Ventline, D. Min.
January 11, 2013

About the Author

A native of Detroit, the writer, pastor, counselor and personal fitness trainer, is a board certified professional counselor.

He earned his doctor of ministry degree at St. Mary's Seminary and University, Baltimore, MD. Recipient of the Detroit, MI., Human Rights Unsung Hero Award, Father Ventline was awarded the Stewart Kerr Ecumenical Award. A jogger, he enjoys cooking, and, leads Holy Humor groups.